# Note to Parents and Teachers

The SCIENCE STARTERS series introduces key science vocabulary to young children while encouraging them to discover and understand the world around them. The series works as a set of graded readers in three levels.

LEVEL 1: BEGINNING TO READ
These books can be read alone or as part of guided or group reading.
Each book has three sections:

• Information pages that introduce new words. These key words appear in bold throughout the book for easy recognition.
• A lively story that recalls this vocabulary and encourages children to use these words when they talk and write.
• A quiz and word search ask children to look back and recall what they have read.

IS IT ALIVE? looks at LIVING THINGS. Below are some answers and activities related to the questions on the information spreads that parents, carers, and teachers can use to discuss and develop further ideas and concepts:

p. 7 *What things are alive but do not move much?* Plants are alive but move very slowly—many flowers close their petals at night and open wide in the morning. Some animals move slowly and may stay still for a long time, such as snails and limpets.

p. 9 *What other ways do animals move?* Encourage children to widen vocabulary using words like scuttle, slither, crawl, or hop. You could ask them to act out the movements.

p. 11 *What do you need to be strong and healthy?* As well as good food and plenty of water, our bodies need fresh air, exercise, rest, and a good night's sleep.

p. 13 *What can you see, hear, smell, and feel in a park?* Encourage children to explore with their senses in a park or garden. They can see and hear insects and birds, smell the flowers, or feel the rough trunk of a tree or a soft clump of grass or moss.

p. 15 *How can you tell that you are growing?* As we grow we get taller and heavier—that's why we grow out of our clothes and shoes. Our nails and hair grow too.

p. 17 *What does a plant need to live and grow?* As well as nutrients from the soil (food) and water, plants need lots of sunlight to help them grow.

p. 21 *Why does a truck need a driver?* A driver starts and stops the engine and steers the truck (so it does not bump into things). A truck can't do these things by itself.

p. 23 *Seashells were once alive. Where can you find them?* You find shells on the beach. They once grew on the backs of animals such as clams, limpets, and mussels.

---

## ADVISORY TEAM

Educational Consultant
**Andrea Bright**—Science Coordinator, Trafalgar Junior School

Literacy Consultant
**Jackie Holderness**—former Principal Lecturer in Primary Education, Westminster Institute, Oxford Brookes University

Series Consultants
**Anne Fussell**—Early Years Teacher and University Tutor, Westminster Institute, Oxford Brookes University

**David Fussell**—C.Chem., FRSC

# CONTENTS

© Aladdin Books Ltd 2007

**Designed and produced by**
Aladdin Books Ltd

**First published in**
the United States in 2007 by
Stargazer Books
c/o The Creative Company
123 South Broad Street
P.O. Box 227
Mankato, Minnesota 56002

Printed in the United States
All rights reserved

**Editor:** Jim Pipe
**Design:** Flick, Book Design
and Graphics
**Picture Research:**
Alexa Brown

Thanks to:
• The pupils of Trafalgar Infants School
and Armen, Zara, and Mia Babasyan, and
Aran Vartanyan for appearing as models.
• Debbie Staynes for helping to organize
the photoshoots, and the pupils and
teachers of Trafalgar Junior School and
St. Nicholas C.E. Infant School for testing
the sample books.

Library of Congress Cataloging-in-
Publication Data

Hewitt, Sally, 1949-
   Living things / by Sally Hewitt.
    p. cm. -- (Science starters. Level 1)
    ISBN 978-1-59604-082-3
   1. Life (Biology)--Juvenile
   literature. I. Title. II. Series.

QH501.H493 2006
570--dc22
              2005056018

Photocredits:
l-left, r-right, b-bottom, t-top,
c-center, m-middle
Front cover tl, tm & tr, 5t, 10br,
23t, 31tr, 32br — Photodisc.
Front cover b, 2bl, 7t, 8, 22bl,
31ml, 32mlt — Marc
Arundale/Select Pictures. 2tl, 6t,
18, 19t — TongRo. 2ml, 11l, 15tr,
16, 32mrt, 32mr — USDA. 3,
15b, 31mr — US Fish & Wildlife
Service. 4, 13tr, 14, 32tr — Digital
Vision. 5br, 17tr, 24tl & mr,
25mr, 26 both, 27mr & bl, 28br,
29bl, 30, 32mlb — Jim Pipe. 6br,
12, 22tr, 24bl &br, 27t, 28tl, 29tr,
32ml, 32tr — Comstock. 7br, 8tl,
11r, 17b, 19br, 20, 32mrb —
Corbis. 8m — Stockbyte. 8br,
10m — John Foxx Images. 13b —
Corel. 21, 31bl, 32bl — Scania.
25bl — Ingram Publishing.

SCIENCE STARTERS

LEVEL

# LIVING THINGS
## Is It
# Alive?

by Sally Hewitt

Stargazer Books

You are **alive**.

You move about.

You eat and drink.

You see and taste and feel.

You are an **animal** called a human.
**Animals** are **alive**.

A **plant** is not
an **animal**,
but a **plant** is
**alive** too.

• What plants and animals can you think of?

The boy is alive.
But sand is **not alive**.

The kitten is alive too.
But a ball of string is **not alive**.

6

These things are **not alive**.

A toy mouse can't move unless you pull the string.

A ball doesn't move until you kick it.

• What things are alive but do not move much?

Things that are alive can **move**.

People can **walk**, run, and jump.
How else can you **move**?

Animals **move** in all kinds of ways.

Fish **swim**.

Birds **fly**.

How does a snail **move**?

• What other ways do animals move?

An animal needs **food** and **water**.
So do plants.

You need **food** and **water**.
They give you **energy** to
move and grow.

10

A goat eats leaves and branches.
A lion hunts for meat to eat.

• What do you need to be strong and healthy?

Things that are alive can **sense**
the world around them.

You can see the dog.
You can feel its soft fur.
What can the dog smell and taste?

A frog has big eyes
to see all around.

A wild cat's
big ears hear
small sounds.

• What can you see, hear, smell, and feel in a park?

13

Things that are alive **grow**.

Animals have **young**.
**Young grow** up to look
like their parents.

You **grow** into an adult.

A piglet **grows** into a pig.

A chick **grows**
into a bird.

• How can you tell that you are growing?

Plants are alive. They take food and water from the soil.

Plants can't walk, swim, or fly, but they do move.

Sunflowers turn their heads to the sun.

A **seed** grows into a plant.

A little acorn is a **seed**.
It grows into
a big oak tree.

• What does a plant need to live and grow?

Look at this picture. What is alive?

People play in the water.
Fish swim in the **sea**. They are alive.

The **sea** moves up and down the
beach, but the **sea** is not alive.

**Trees** move in the wind.
**Trees** are plants, so they are alive.

The wind blows
**clouds** across the sky.

But **clouds** are
not alive.

• What other living things are in the sea?

**Machines** can move and make things.

But **machines** do not eat like us.
They do not grow.

**Machines** are not alive.

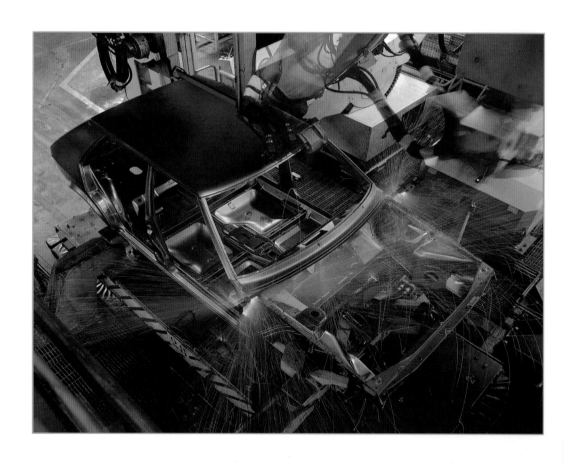

A big truck is a **machine**.
An **engine** helps it move fast.

But a truck can't move by itself.
It needs a driver.

• Why does a truck need a driver?

This baseball bat is made of wood. Wood comes from a tree.

The wood was **once alive**, but the bat is not alive!

A wool scarf was **once alive**.

Wool is hair cut from a sheep.

22

This fossil was **once alive**.

It is an animal that was alive millions of years ago.

We know about dinosaurs from fossils.

• *Seashells were once alive. Where can you find them?*

# TAKING CARE OF TEDDY

Look for words about **living things**.

My friend Millie and her family are on vacation. Dad, Joss, and I **walk** over to their house.

We have to feed the cat, Smoky, and the goldfish, Flash, and **water** the **plants**.

Our dog, Bluey, wants to come too!

24

"Millie has left Teddy behind!" I say.
"Let's take care of Teddy," says Joss.
"He can keep Leo
the lion company!"

"We'll take care of
the **animals** and
**plants** first,"
says Dad.

"Why?" I ask.

"Because they are
**alive**. Teddy is **not**
**alive**. Nor is Leo."

"How do you know Teddy and Leo are **not alive**?" I ask.
I give Teddy a cuddle.

"Teddy and Leo
don't eat and drink,"
says Dad.

"We do!" we say.
"That's because you
are **alive**," laughs Dad.

"Smoky needs to eat
and drink," says Dad.

"Just like Bluey," I say.

26

Dad gives Smoky **food**
to eat and milk to drink.

Joss gives Flash some
**food**. Flash **swims** up and eats it.

We **water** the **plants**.

Joss looks out of the window.
He says, "It's raining!"

"That will **water** the **plants**
outside," says Dad. "They need a drink."

27

"Look," says Dad. "Smoky is **moving** in that bag. He can **sense** something."

"I can **move**, and so can Teddy!" I say. "So can Leo!" says Joss.

We make the toys **fly**.

"But toys can't **move** all by themselves," says Dad.

Smoky sits in the window. He watches the **clouds** and **trees**.

"If I take care of Teddy, will he **grow** big and strong like me?" I ask.

"No," says Dad. "Teddy won't **grow**."

"But Millie will be pleased you are taking care of him."

"And Millie's mom will be pleased we are taking care of Smoky, Flash, and the **plants**," says Jess.

"And I'm pleased I'm taking care of you!" says Dad.

Things that are **alive** like you can:

- **Move**
- **Feel**
- **Eat and drink**
- **Grow**

Snail

Draw pictures of things that are **alive**. Check that they do all these things.

# QUIZ

Are you a **plant** or an **animal**?

Answer on page 5

Is a toy mouse **alive**?

Answer on page 7

What will a chick **grow** into?

Answer on page 15

How do you know
a **machine** is not **alive**?

Answer on page 20-21

Did you know the answers? Give yourself a

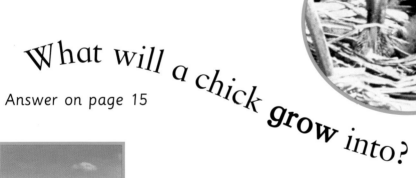

Do you remember these words about **living things**?
Well done! Can you remember any more?

 alive
page 4

not alive
page 6

 move
page 8

food
page 11

 sense
page 12

grow
page 15

 seed
page 17

cloud
page 19

 machine
page 21

once alive
page 23